Emotional Eating and Its Implications

Understanding How Emotional Eating Affects Your Health

Andre Simpson

Copyright and Disclaimer

We support copyright of all intellectual property. Copyright protection continues to spark the seed of creativity in content producers, ensures that everyone has their voice heard through the power of words and the captivity of a story. Uniqueness of culture and content has been passed down through generations of writing and is the DNA of every intelligent species on our planet.

This publication is intended to provide helpful and informative material. It is not intended to diagnose, treat, cure, or prevent any health problem or condition, nor is intended to replace the advice of a physician. No action should be taken solely on the contents of this book. Always consult your physician or qualified health-care professional on any matters regarding your health and before adopting any suggestions in this book or drawing inferences from it.

The author and publisher specifically disclaim all responsibility for any liability, loss or risk, personal or otherwise, which is incurred as a consequence, directly or indirectly, from the use or application of any contents of this book.

Any and all product names referenced within this book are the trademark of their respective owners. None of these owners have sponsored, authorized, endorsed, or approved this book.

Always read all information provided by the manufacturers' product labels before using their products. The author and publisher are not responsible for claims made by manufacturers.

Copyright © 2015

DIGITAL EDITION

Any and all product names referenced within this book are the trademark of their respective owners. None of these owners have sponsored, authorized, endorsed, or approved this book.

What You Will Learn In This Book

How This Book Will Help You and Why

This text is for any individual that is an emotional eater, suspect that they may be emotional eaters or suspect that someone they know may be an emotional eater. The author goes to great lengths to define what emotional eating is and to outline all the signs and symptoms that are associated with the disorder.

Many persons find that they eat even when they are not hungry and they simply cannot figure out why. This book explains all of that and more including highlighting other types of eating disorders other than the emotional.

Dive Right into the Book! Or Learn a Bit More About the Author

ABOUT THE AUTHOR

Andre Simpson has had his own battle with emotional eating. He was born in Delaware and moved to Chicago when he was ten years old when his father got a better paying job. He struggled to make new friends and as a result he succumbed to food to quell his depression. Soon he was overweight and on the verge of becoming morbidly obese. Something had to be done. His parents along with a professional helped him to come to terms with his feelings and to fight his cravings. Now he spends his tiem helping others who are going through similar problems.

The book will appeal to the reader as it not only highlights the problems but provides viable solutions as well.

Table of Contents

Copyright and Disclaimer

What You Will Learn In This Book

About The Author

Words To The Wise

Introduction

It Starts with Food Cravings

Chapter One

   Why People Eat When They Are Depressed or Stressed

Chapter Two

   Can You Fight the Hunger?

   Emotional Hunger and Physical Hunger

   Food Cravings – The Uncontrollable Demon

Chapter Three

   In-Depth Look at Emotional Eating

   Overcoming Emotional Eating

   Are You an Emotional Eater? – The Symptoms

Chapter Four

   Beating Emotional Eating In Three Stages

   Stage 1 – Discipline and Denial

   Stage 2 – The Exercise Regimen

   Stage 3 – Speeding Up Your Metabolism

   Stage 4 – Snack Attacks

   Stage 5 – Smoothie World

Chapter Five

Other Dangerous Eating Disorders

Overeating

What Are the Signs and Symptoms of an Overeater?

What Are The Effects Of Compulsive Overeating?

Is It an Addiction and What Help Should One Get?

Food Addiction

Compulsive Eating & Fixing It

Words To The Wise

"I suffered from eating disorders when I was just a kid. I did not like me or the way I looked. But back then, you could not tell anyone."

- **Richard Simmons**

INTRODUCTION

IT STARTS WITH FOOD CRAVINGS

This is such an important topic I decided to make it the starting point of the book – cravings lead to overeating, food addiction and emotional eating all rolled into one!

Food cravings are one of the reasons why many people on a dieting program fail. When on a diet, it is very common for us to experience cravings for some of our favorite meals. In simple terms, food cravings are the excess desires for more nutrients by the body. In most cases, people tend to crave for what they like eating most. This is a condition that can result in the consumption of the wrong types of food simply because the body is yearning for them. Food cravings can have a very adverse effect on the body if they are not dealt with and it is therefore important to learn how to survive food cravings.

One of the ways to survive food cravings is by identifying the foods that trigger the cravings. As defined earlier, food cravings are usually desires by the body for more nutrients. In most cases, people tend to crave for their most favorite meals and it is therefore important to minimize the intake of such foods. In addition, sugary foods such as chocolates and snacks can also trigger cravings and as such they should be avoided.

Another reason why we can experience food cravings is due to the reduction of blood sugar levels in the body. As soon as the blood sugar levels drop in the body, a signal is sent to the brain alerting it to the body's need for more sugar. As a result, a craving for more food is triggered. Although the blood sugar levels can trigger cravings, it is important to maintain a good and healthy diet. In this case, it is important to have an intake of food supplements that have low sugar concentrations. The meals you consume should contain low sugar concentrations. Through the consumption of such foods, you are not only sure of natural and healthy weight loss but also stable blood sugar levels to reduce the cravings.

To avoid food cravings and maintain a healthy eating habit, it is advisable to maintain a healthy eating schedule composed of foods with low fat and sugar levels. In some cases, cravings for certain foods can be emotional and it is therefore important to determine whether your cravings are as a result of different moods and body reactions such as stress and depression. Once you feel the food cravings, it is advisable to drink of some water to stave off the craving.

Chapter One

Reasons Why Most Diets Fail – Stress!

There have been many cases where a person starts a diet only to find that it is not working. They end up giving up on the diet and stating it is a failure. This happens a lot and there are many reasons why a diet fails and why people have issues going down this path. Let's take a look at some of the key reasons for why diets fail and why it is important to have the right approach to make sure this does not become a regular habit. It is fine to make one mistake, but to make many shows signs of weakness.

Incomplete Diet

It is essential to know that there are going to be some diets that are just not good enough and are 'incomplete'. These are the diets that might come across as fads and are just trying to get consumers to purchase and try them out before fading away. Go with tried and tested diets because those are the only ones worth trying.

Half-Hearted Approach

There are many people who decide to get started on a diet only to realize that they do not want to make the effort that is required. They will start to slip and that is the first sign that the diet is going to fall apart in a hurry and positive results will never be achieved. It is essential to be committed to any diet because that is the only way to get the results that you desire. A half-hearted approach is going to lead to half-hearted results. It does not matter what diet is being followed at that point.

No Additional Work

The final reason why diets fail has to do with the lack of supplementary work that is done by those on the diet. For example, a person that is on a diet should be doing some form of exercise too. If a person is sitting on their hands all day and not doing anything but following the diet, the results are not going to be as optimized as they could have been with a bit of exercise.

These are three of the biggest reasons why diets tend to fail. It is important to do your research before moving on and making sure that you are committed to the task at hand. Those who are committed and have the right diet in place will see results.

Why People Eat When They Are Depressed or Stressed

Eating when stressed, or depressed is just part of the bigger picture of emotional eating. The habits see many people deal with the problems having a craving for food and eating large quantities of it for reasons other than satiating hunger.

Compulsive overeating is the adverse outcome of such uncontrolled eating behavior. So what are the reasons for such a disorder?

Research links the issues to a particular chemical in the brain. The brain tends to release chemicals called endorphins that I control the moods and energy levels. Endorphins also called the "happy chemical" are released when one is activate (exercising) or when excited, the same excitement when doing something fun like having sex, or eating delicious foods.

With that in mind, fits of depression, angers, stress, and other emotional triggers will cause the mind to release a chemical that will cause a person to desire eating food that they love. These foods are termed as comfort foods, dishes they eat to make them feel better. The food is a "quick fix" as the use of drugs would be to a drug junky.

Some of the triggers that cause people to eat when they are stressed, or depressed include:

I. *Situational Triggers* – These triggers tend to pop up based on time and place. For instance, the person might be in a restaurant or just might be passing by a food court and the smell triggers the mind to think of particular foods. If the person has a stressful day or is depressed, the smell will trigger the mind to think of food that makes the persons feel happy or excited.
II. *Social Triggers* – They are typically the result of interactions with people. It is easier for most people to eat more than need when around other people. Stressed or depressed people do not easily mingle with people but if the right triggers are present, in this case food, they will eat just to fit in. Theirs will be eating to overshadow their feeling or low self-worth and other inadequacies when they are around other people.
III. *Emotional Triggers* – many people who overeat do so due to underlying emotional problems. Issues of emotional pain, anxiety, emotional stress, depression, anger, boredom are all easy elements that trigger compulsive eating in some people.

Each of the above categories is linked to the release of endorphins in the brain, that aid in the control of moods, feelings, and energy. However, people who rarely overeat experience a burst of energy after eating since their chief reason for eating is to deal with an emotional problem.

Chapter Two

Can You Fight the Hunger?

Emotional Hunger and Physical Hunger

Emotional eating can be termed as a disorder which causes an individual to consume large amounts of food in response to negative emotions instead of hunger. When one realizes that food can offer comfort, he/she immediately turns to food for short term healing of emotional distress. Every now and then, we will consume large quantities of food during thanksgiving for instance, but when this eating becomes uncontrollable then it obviously becomes a problem.

Have you found yourself in kitchen looking for a snack even when you aren't hungry? Or maybe eating a whole container of ice-cream just because you are hungry? If that is the case then you are most likely going through a phase of emotional eating disorder. To know whether you have an eating disorder or not, you will first have to realize the basic differences between emotional eating and eating out of hunger. At first, it can be hard to admit especially if you use food to resolve your emotions but it is a paramount step in treating emotional eating.

So, what is the difference between emotional hunger and physical hunger?

To begin with, emotional hunger is rapid and comes suddenly opposed to physical hunger which comes gradually over time throughout the day.

Emotional hunger prompts urgent satisfaction compared to physical hunger which can wait until it is convenient to eat.

Emotional hunger will only lead to the craving of specific types of food commonly referred to as 'comfort foods' while physical hunger will always be open to a wide variety of foods. In the latter, lots of things usually sound delicious or good.

Physical hunger usually stops when one is full unlike emotional hunger where one continues to eat even when full. This regular eating is meant to comfort the individual during emotional distress and not satisfy hunger.

Eating in response to negative emotions will often result to feelings of regret, shame and guilt when one is done eating. In real hunger, one is usually left satisfied, at ease and happy. Treating emotional eating disorder can indeed be a huge challenge, but it all begins with admitting that there is a problem.

Food Cravings – The Uncontrollable Demon

Once people become food junkies, they never want to accept the truth. They would rather withdraw from social circles and seek comfort in food. Truth be told; many binge eaters just let their cravings take the better of them. It is no secret that cravings can be relentless prowlers that can strike fast and hard.

Taking control of the craving is a good place to start to keep you from becoming a food junky. Here are a few tips that you might want to consider if you are battling food cravings.

It Is a Mental Game You Must Win

The first step to gain control of the cravings is to understand and appreciate that your mind will be playing games on you. Hence, you need to take charge and win at the game. Appreciate that the cravings are just a state of though, and thus be affirmative with your actions. Tell yourself you know you are not hungry, and you do not have to eat every time you think about food.

Take Note of the Triggers

It is good to always assess your eating habits. Take note of the foods that act as triggers. At times, you might smell or eat a certain food that might trigger a craving for another type of food. At other times, it might be something you are doing or thinking about that is the trigger. Learn to identify the triggers and avoid them as all costs.

Take Part in Activities

The mind will always take charge when the body is not engaged in other activities. In short, keeping yourself busy will help the mind to focus on what you are doing and not on food. Simple daily chores around the house or the workplace will be a good distraction.

Eat With a Set Plan

The cravings aim to make you eat when you think of food. You can counter this by developing a plan on what to eat and when. You will have to give in to the cravings at some point, which is important to limit any emotional and psychological stress. However, only give in once at the last point and ensure that you take small portions of what you crave for substituting the rest with other foods. Remember to take just the right portions of food. Do Not OVEREAT.

Always Share With Others

One of the strangest things about food junkies is that they never want to share their food. Cravings will always make you see the food as a small quantity that cannot be shared. The result of this is eating more that you should. Just get the food and share it among your friends, it will help to prevent this and even be the better person when the cravings strike.

Root Causes of Emotional Eating

Emotional eating is really the habit where one eats large amounts of food, not because he/she is hungry, but due to an emotional breakdown. Although there are many factors that lead to emotional eating, most culprits do so due to stress. Medical researchers also link emotional eating to hormonal imbalances, especially when adrenal glands release too much cortisol due to stress. Discussed below are the most common causes of emotional eating.

1. *Sugar or Fat Cravings*: This is the number one cause for emotional eating. Most of the people who suffer from this condition prefer sugary foods and fries for satisfaction. Eating such sugary and fatty foods however doesn't satisfy their needs. This is due to the fact that such cravings are induced when the body releases insulin, cortisol and ghrelin (hunger hormones) in excess.
2. *Social Eating*: Some people, especially women, turn to emotional eating when down or stressed out about something. Ladies have a tendency of ordering more food than they need when with their 'girlfriends', thus eating too much. This habit doesn't however extend past the social grounds as many people get back to their 'busy' lives.

3. *Nervousness*: Most people tend to eat more when alone, nervous or when anxious about something. The nervous breakdown makes them chew anything in their hands, starting with their fingernails. Some will even go to a greater extent of buying chips and fries, or even take on canned foods for comfort. The only way to overcome such nervousness and anxiety is by learning how to remain calm, or even talk a walk when the cravings strike.
4. *Physiological Eating*: This mostly happens if one has skipped several meals. Skipping meals causes intense hunger, which forces the person to consume any foods he/she comes across for satisfaction. Although this only goes for a few hours, some people may continue to eat even after their stomach is full.
5. *Situational Eating*: This habit is very common with children. This habit sets in when one sees an advertisement of a delicacy/food he/she loves and is then inclined to buy. Watching the TV, movies or even attending a sporting event can trigger emotional eating. Most people do not realize they are eating too much until they are told.

Although emotional eating is an acquired habit, one can work around it and stop overeating completely. Identifying the reasons why you overeat even when not hungry, such as stress, situational and even physiological factors can help you quit the behavior. Learning how to manage stress can also help you quit the habit altogether.

Chapter Three

In-Depth Look at Emotional Eating

Do you resort to food whenever you feel angry, stressed out, tired or sad? Do you usually turn to eating whenever you feel bored, or does it give you a different kind of satisfaction? If you do, don't fret – many people turn to food for the same reasons that you do. However, if you have the urge to eat not because you're hungry, but because you only wanted to, this can be defined as emotional eating and it can be a problem.

Aside from the fact that emotional eating can lead to weight gain or even obesity, it can even cause further problems such as high blood pressure, diabetes and other health conditions. Some people just feel happy after eating – they were able to find comfort in food, but this doesn't make it okay just to indulge in eating food whenever they wanted to. As mentioned in previous chapters, emotional eating has to be stopped as soon as possible. Many people are not even aware of this problem. As a matter of fact, many individuals do not even they gradually gain weight making it an ever bigger problem.

Overcoming Emotional Eating

Perform a self-assessment, and if you answer yes to all of the questions mentioned above, then you have to do something about it. The great thing is, there are a lot of ways that you can do to help yourself. One way of doing so is being kind to yourself.

As soon as you have realized that you are turning to food just for anything to comfort you, try and give yourself a little bit of a break. It may be tough, but be conscious of these things and as soon as you have noticed that you're turning to food again for other reasons than being physical hungry, then stop. You can control yourself – think of the possible effects that this can have if you don't do something about it.

Aside from self-control, you can also seek external help. There is professional help that you can get, to help you get over this problem. Additionally, you can even seek your friends' help. Do something fun – be engaged in different activities and make yourself busy. This way, you can get away from the thought of eating, which plays an important role in helping you get rid of the problem.

Emotional eating might not sound like a big deal for most people- but if not attended to as soon as possible, your health may suffer. As early as now, make your move and do something – other people were able to do so, and you can too.

Are You an Emotional Eater? – The Symptoms

For binge eaters, overeating is constant and uncontrollable which eventually results to overweight problems. The disorder is basically projected by compulsive overeating, whereby an individual consumes large amounts of food every now and then when in emotional distress. One will notice the symptoms of the eating disorder during late adolescence or young adulthood. An emotional eating occurrence will usually last around two or three hours but for some, the episodes will occur all day long in frequencies. The symptoms can however be categorized into two; emotional symptoms and behavioral symptoms.

Some of the known behavioral symptoms of emotional eating disorder include;

- The inability to resist the urge to eat or control what you are eating.
- The rapid consumption of large amounts of food every now and then.
- Consumption of adequate quantities of food even when full.
- Hiding food for later consumption in secrecy.
- Continuous consumption of food throughout the day without any meal schedules.
- Eating because opportunity has arisen. For instance, passing by a restaurant and eating because of seeing and advertisement of a particular serving.

Emotional symptoms of the disorder include:

- Feeling of tension and distress that can only be relieved by eating.

- ❖ Eating as a result of negative thoughts on self-worth and esteem.
- ❖ Regular periods of embarrassment over how much food you are consuming.
- ❖ Desperation to resolve the bad eating habits and weight issues emanating from the disorder.
- ❖ Out-of-earth feeling while eating to deal with the negative emotions.
- ❖ Lack of satisfaction regardless of how much or what you eat.

In essence, it is important to realize that this eating disorder can lead to a host of emotional, physical and social issues. According to various research, individuals with emotional eating disorder often report more health issues, insomnia and suicidal thoughts compared to those without the disorder. It is therefore paramount that you seek professional help, immediately you relate with the symptoms above. There are several help and support groups in most locations that work at tackling the disorder.

Notable Social Changes

The reasons for binge eating will differ between persons, and can at times be due to a genetic predisposition. Most binge eating is however, due to cultural, social and environmental factors, and quite often a result of emotional disturbances. It can occur in people of all ages, with no discrimination of gender, and has no connection with any cultural background, or belonging to any particular socioeconomic group.

Eating Quickly

Most binge eaters tend to eat very quickly, and will do their eating even when they are not in the least bit hungry. They will continue to eat even when they are fully sated. Most people with this disorder always feel guilty or ashamed of their habit, but are unable to control it. Binge eating is quite often a sign of boredom, or a sign of a distress that a person is emotionally not able to cope with. They can be triggered by wanting to suppress emotions or other inability to deal with situations.

Can't Sleep At Night and Are Very Lethargic

Most binge eaters will have trouble sleeping and will always feel tired. They may develop intolerance to certain foods, and will feel constantly constipated and bloated. They are people who are always preoccupied with food, while also being aware of their weight and shape.

They will feel dissatisfied about their bodies and ashamed about the way they appear to others. Every episode of binge eating does have them feeling guilty, sad, anxious and distressed. They generally have a low opinion about themselves. You will always find them irritable, anxious and depressed. They are highly sensitive to any comments made about their habit, the food they eat and their own weight and probable lack of exercise.

Acting Very Cagey and Secretive

Binge eaters will be secretive about anything relating to food, and will probably have their own secret hordes of food. They will avoid answering all questions regarding their weight and what they eat. They may even withdraw from all previous activities and become increasingly isolated. Their behavior can be erratic and they may spend a lot of money on food, while those without the means to do so may even do some shoplifting. There are chances that they will harm themselves, indulge in substance abuse and may want to commit suicide. Binge eating can lead to serious health disorders, mainly a result of unchecked weight.

Chapter Four

Beating Emotional Eating In Three Stages

Stage 1 – Discipline and Denial

In reality, there are many ways you can stop eating more than you need. Specifically, stop eating too much junk, fat, sugar, and carbs that are making you bloat. Don't believe ME? Here is what worked for me in this 3 step plan.

1. Put the Food Away

We tend to forget we even have certain snacks if they're not right in front of our face. Sadly, most of us have a habit of keeping the snacks right on the counter, or even worse, in our desks! Get rid of them now and put them where they belong - deep in the pantry or up high in a cupboard.

2. Get Rid Of the Associations

Most people eat when they're bored. They'll eat when they're watching TV or playing a game because it makes them feel good. Get rid of these habits right now. You don't need a bag of chips when you watch a late show or play a co-op game. In fact, how are you even benefiting from it if you don't remember eating it?

3. Distract Yourself

If you're getting close to meal time but have the munchies, it may be tempting to load up on chips, cookies, or other junk. Instead, distract yourself with something that commands all of your attention, such as a favorite TV show or reading a book. If you're at work, this can be easy to do - simply concentrate on your work! Eventually you will train your brain to stop giving into so many cravings.

4. Portion Control

Okay, so we talked about junk food... how about emotional eating at meal time? This is a big area where people eat too much. The answer is simple: practice good portion control and eat slowly!

Start with half the normal portion than you usually eat. Remember, you can get more later. Yet you may be surprised at how filling that smaller portion may be. Just be sure to eat slowly so your stomach can tell your brain it's full before you eat more than you can chew.

Dedicating yourself to stop emotional eating is an admirable thing. Good luck, and save your appetite for the good stuff!

Stage 2 – The Exercise Regimen

I wanted to get rid of at least 1000 calories daily when I was at home and the easiest way was to do one or more of these exercises for one hour every day. These are great cardiovascular activities that are going to get the heart racing and ensure that you are shedding the excess fat along with those calories in no time.

Treadmill

The first place and what most people do is head toward the treadmill. You can set different speeds and simply run in the same spot in order to burn as many calories as you need. This can be highly effective for those who do not want to get creative with their approach while still getting the type of results that they want. It is a proven method and those who vary their speeds are going to get a lot more out of the exercise than those who do not. Learn to vary the speeds to maximize the workout.

Stationary Bike

This is similar to heading towards the treadmill for those who do have stationary bikes. This is once again a fantastic piece of equipment that is going to help burn a lot of calories at home. If you do have a bike at home, this is the best thing to hop onto and burn a few calories quick. The best part about getting on a bike is that you can pace yourself as you want. If you want to burn more calories, put in more effort and do it for longer periods of time.

Jumping Jacks

It is now time to look at exercises that are great for those who do not have any equipment. Jumping jacks are great because the goal is to do as many as you can and do them as fast as you can. Make sure the hands are hitting each other with the completion of the movement. You will start to notice how your heart rate increases in a hurry.

Mountain Climbers

You want something that is going to put pressure on the entire body? Mountain climbers are the way to go. The goal is to get hunched into a runner's position (as you see before races) and then push each leg towards the elbows.

Lunges and High Knees

The final exercise comes in the form of lunges. Try to mix them up with high knees to get better results. This will put a lot of pressure on the body and burn those calories.

Stage 3 – Speeding Up Your Metabolism

I knew I had to change what I was eating – but what if it what I was eating could help me lose weight. Although genetics mainly governs body metabolism, several factors can be used to accelerate it up. An increase in body metabolism means the body will be able to respire more fats, hence facilitate weight loss and a great body figure. Although most people prefer indulging in anaerobic exercises to induce increased body metabolism, there are foods that can help with more than just that. Adding these foods in your diet can boost body metabolism to higher rates than the most intense workouts can achieve

Some of these foods include:

Green Tea: Green tea is a great source of antioxidants and polyphenols. Polyphenols are compounds that help boost body metabolism and improves the heart's health. In addition to this, green tea contains phytonutrients that help detox the body thus facilitating proper health.

Oatmeal: Oatmeal is an excellent source of insoluble fiber. Insoluble fiber is important in the body as it helps reduce toxicity along the gut and enhances the body's ability to fight cancerous cells. Insoluble fiber is however hard to digest, meaning the body is forced to trigger an increased metabolism to digest the same. More fats are respired to provide energy for the increased metabolic rates, thus facilitating weight loss.

Turkey: One of the main reasons why most people love turkey is for its nutritional benefits. To begin with, turkey is a great source of high-quality proteins and very low in fats (without the skin of course). The best thing about turkey meat is that, it's rich in compounds that boost body metabolism. It also contains compounds that help the body relax, which is the reason why most people feel sleepy after a satisfying meal of turkey. Aside from improving body metabolism, the body's immunity and ability to regulate blood pressure is improved.

Green Leafy Vegetables (Spinach): Green leafy vegetables are packed with vitamins, nutrients and phytonutrients that are highly beneficial to the body. Spinach, for example, helps improve the body's ability to fight oxidative stress, as well as inhibits aging in most people. It is also packed with both soluble and insoluble fiber. The central importance of soluble fiber is that it helps slow down starch digestion while insoluble fiber facilitates food movement along the gut along many other functions. By reducing the digestion of carbs, the body is forced to turn to fats to supplement energy thus an increase in metabolism occurs.

Other foods that do improve body metabolic rates include grapes, berries, whey proteins and almonds.

Stage 4 – Snack Attacks

Refraining from binge eating is hard work – I mean it's real easy to backslide. So I developed some 100 calorie recipes that I devoured until I was able to resist temptation (the cravings went after about 3 days)

Great Snack Recipes below 100 Calories

Banana Muffins Recipe

The snack is delicious and very nutritious as it contains low sugar and fat, especially if fat-free sour cream is used.

Ingredients – (12 servings);

1 cup of all-purpose flour

A quarter tablespoon baking soda

A quarter cup white sugar

One egg

A quarter cup sour cream

One cup mashed banana (ripe)

A quarter teaspoon vanilla extract

One tablespoon of baking powder

A quarter teaspoon salt

How to prepare;

Begin by preheating the oven to 350 degrees as you embark on greasing muffin cups or lining using paper muffin liners.

In one bowl, mix together the flour, salt, baking powder, and baking soda. In the other, beat together the egg, vanilla, banana and sugar as you stir in the sour cream. Once this is done, pour in the latter mixture into the flour as you stir until it is completely combined. Now scoop the mixture as you batter into the muffin cups.

Bake the muffins in the preheated oven for 15 to 20 minutes then let them cool before serving.

Garlic Pita Bread Bites Recipe

A popular choice and a favorite of people who not only enjoy healthy snacks, but delicious ones too

Ingredients – (20 servings);

1 teaspoon crushed garlic

2 tablespoons grated Parmesan cheese

3 tablespoons butter

1 teaspoon dried Italian seasoning

1 package pita bread cut in half

How to prepare;

Begin by preheating the oven to 350 degrees, and then open both halves of the pita bread prior to cutting them into 2 inch pieces. Arrange these pieces on a baking sheet.

Place a sauce pan over medium heat to melt the butter and the mix in the dried Italian seasoning and garlic. Pour this mixture over the pita bread pieces.

Now sprinkle the bread with the cheese, and then bake in the preheated oven for 10 minutes until lightly browned.

Baked Kale Chips Recipe

Like potato chips, these chips are very addictive. The easy-to-make snack is however much more nutritious with low calories.

Ingredients – (6 servings);

1 tablespoon olive oil

1 bunch kale

1 teaspoon seasoned salt

How to prepare;

Begin by preheating the oven to 350 degrees while you line a non-insulated cookie sheet preferably with parchment paper.

Remove the kale leaves from the stems using a knife prior to tearing these leaves into bite sized pieces. After washing and drying, season the salt and drizzle over the olive oil.

Bake inside the preheated oven until the edges of the bites turn brown but not brunt. This will usually take 10 to 15 minutes.

Stage 5 – Smoothie World

If you're like most people, you're probably wondering if smoothies can indeed help with weight loss. And the answer to that question is yes, smoothies can make you lose weight. They do it by providing the body with all the necessary nutrients while cutting down on the unwanted calories. I binged on smoothies starting out at almost 3 cups a day – I was full in minutes. So this worked wonders along with the 100 Calorie Snacks.

If you know how to make the right smoothie, you could have the right balance of complex carbohydrates, proteins, healthy fats, and vitamins and minerals.

There are many kinds of smoothies out there, and not all of them are created alike. There are certain smoothies that do a better job of making you lose weight than others. There are also certain ingredients that you can add to your smoothie to make your smoothie better.

You could, for example, add some avocado to make your smoothie extra creamy. Avocados are rich in healthy fat, which will make you feel full until your next meal. Plus it contains different nutrients.

Berries also make a good addiction to any smoothie. They add more flavor without adding extra calories or simple sugars. They are rich in fiber which, like avocado, helps you to feel full until your next meal. They are also rich in anti-oxidants for good health.

Cayenne pepper is a spicy smoothie addition that boosts your body's ability to lose weight because of a compound called capsaicin. Research shows that adding cayenne pepper to your breakfast reduces your consumption of carbohydrates and fat later in the day. When stated another way, consuming some cayenne pepper curbs your appetite.

Chia seeds are a great ingredient for weight loss. They are rich in fiber and protein, which keep you feeling full and satisfied. They are also rich in nutrients like antioxidants, calcium, and omega-3. They're also known to absorb the toxins away from your digestive tract. You will find that many smoothies for dieting make extensive use of Chia seeds.

Cinnamon is a popular spice that you can use to help regulate your blood sugar levels. It boosts the metabolism of glucose. This reduces the amount of excess glucose in your blood, which can be stored as fat. Studies have shown that abdominal fat is more sensitive to cinnamon than fat in other parts of the body.

Coconut oil is the number one ingredient you can add to your smoothie because it contains medium chain fats, which can be easily used by the body for energy.

First Note on Exercise

Exercise and a healthy diet are most essential for physical health, and can also help to improve mental health. When you are more active it does help to relieve stress, feeling of anxiety and lifts you out of depression. It does help you to sleep better and this can keep you in a better frame of mind at all times.

It is not necessary to be a fitness fanatic to get all the mental advantages that can come from exercising. Irrespective of how old you are, or the level of fitness that you are at, exercise can make your life better, especially when you enjoy the physical activities that can lead to an improvement in emotional health. A lot of people exercise because it gives them an enormous sense of well-being. The increased energy levels that do result from exercise, extends into their work life and helps performance, which further increases satisfaction with life. People who exercise regularly will also have sharper memories, because of the good rest they get. They also feel more relaxed and positive about themselves.

Exercise helps to reduce anxiety and stress and tension in life. Your troubles will not vanish when you exercise, but the easing of stress and tension will have you looking at problems in a fresh light and help to find solutions for them. Exercise can lift moods and relieve you of any feeling of being depressed. It helps to sharpen brainpower because of the release of certain hormones that exercise does encourage the production of. For some reason, people who exercise regularly are proud of this habit and it does increase their self-esteem. The improved sleep does lead to more energy and this can help you to cope better with the challenges you are required to confront every day.

A body under stress has tense muscles, especially about the shoulders, neck and face. The worry and distress caused by this discomfort leads to even greater stress. Exercise can help to break this connection, by releasing brain endorphins, while relaxing muscles and thus releasing the tension being felt. The body and mind are closely interlinked, and when the body feels better, it is also going to help the mind to feel better. Stop thinking of exercise as a chore, and do it willingly, till it becomes a habit that the body demands on its own. Find the time to do so, even in a very busy schedule, and you will soon find that it is a part of your schedule that can never be avoided.

Why You Must Make the Change

Remember that eating disorders are broadly viewed as the abnormal eating habits that can endanger your health and life. Eating disorders can be a great issue of concern to people since they not only lead to physical body changes but also emotional changes. Eating disorders mainly fall into four different categories that is bulimia nervosa, anorexia nervosa, binge-eating disorder and eating orders not specified. Among the four disorders, bulimia and anorexia are the most common types since they can be witnessed in people of all age brackets and different gender.

Anorexia – What I Did Not Say

Anorexia is an eating disorder that is characterized by tremendous reduction in eating, in addition, this condition can also be characterized by not eating at all. This can be later accompanied by excessive exercising that goes way beyond just weight loss and dieting. On the other hand, Bulimia is characterized by long periods of secretive eating or binge- eating. The condition is later accompanied by inappropriate weight-control methods such as purging or self-induced vomiting, abuse of laxatives and over exercising. Binge-eating is portrayed by short periods of excessive eating. Eating disorders that are not specified do not specifically fall in one of the above categories but can be a combination of two disorders.

One way in which eating disorders can affect your health is by increasing one's blood pressure. Most of the eating disorders are characterized by high intake of food substances such as sugars, fats and carbohydrates. In the process of this excess eating, an individual may consume large amounts of cholesterol. Once in the human body, the cholesterol gets absorbed into the blood stream where is blocks some of the blood arterioles. As a result, the surface area of the blood vessels decreases contributing to a high blood pressure so that blood can be pumped through the thin vessels. This can even result into some cardiac failures due to constant overworking of the heart.

Another effect of eating disorders on the body is that they can result into some unpredicted psychological disorders. Majority of the people who suffer from eating disorders are in constant though about their fate and ending. As a result of the buildup in thoughts, an individual can develop some psychologically inflicted disorders such as stress, depression and anxiety which can result into drug abuse to try and tone down the feelings.

Chapter Five

Other Dangerous Eating Disorders

Overeating

Almost everyone has overeaten as some point in life. As has been expressed throughout this book overeating can be viewed as a mindless habit where a person eats without being fully conscious of it; for instance, when eating a bag of chips while watching the TV.

Overeating can also be linked a medical condition known as compulsive eating disorder. Other people simply view it as a form of binge-eating. However, the reality of it is that eating more food than needed is something the results from underlying emotional problems such as stress of life, lack of self-appreciation, and negative body image among others.

Overeating will have a direct effect on the person's physiological, emotional, and psychological attributes hence compromising his or her quality of life. In most cases the compulsive eating is more or less like a drug stimulant where the person gets a euphoric feeling just like that of a drug abuser. Eating is how the person lets go of stress, shame, anger, sadness, fear, among other emotional and psychological feelings. It thus suffices to say that people who suffer from compulsive eating disorder have a food obsession that makes them eat even when they are not hungry.

What Are the Signs and Symptoms of an Overeater?

A number of signs are simple indicators that someone is a compulsive overeater. Some of the common signs include:

Not sharing food

Eating food quickly

Secretive eating habits

Feeling of guilt after eating

Depression

Viewing food a close, comforting companion among others

What Are The Effects Of Compulsive Overeating?

The effects of overeating are health related and include:

Cases of obesity

Fatigue

Heart problems

Irregular blood sugar levels

Diabetes

Stroke

Sleep apnea

Arthritis

High cholesterol

Bone deterioration among others

Is It an Addiction and What Help Should One Get?

Research into cases of overeating has proven that the issues are relative to an addiction to food. Studies done on sugar, and salt based foods that show these types of foods are addictive support the finding. Hence, eating more that needs might be as a result of addiction to a variety of foods.

It is rather hard for people suffering from a binge eating disorder (compulsive eating) to quit on their own. The way to help them make positive progress is to help them to seek a medical treatment approach. One particular approach is focusing on unearthing the deep rooted emotional and psychological issues that triggered the overeating problem.

Food Addiction

Just like any other type of addiction, food addiction is an unstoppable impulse to gorge on food, and anyone who suffers from this type of addiction has a compulsive eating habit even when they are not hungry.

What causes food addiction? People who have anorexia, bulimia or some other type of eating disorder may also have food addition. Most of us overindulge in food from time to time especially during the holidays. However, food addicts struggle with binge eating every day. They struggle to control their impulse to eat.

What causes food addiction? How addiction develops is really a complex topic. Alcohol, drugs and food can trigger dopamine release in the brain. If you didn't know it yet, dopamine is the chemical that causes you to feel pleasure. It creates a positive link between emotional well-being and food. In a food-addicted brain, food is look upon as a drug. It's used to recreate the feelings of pleasure, even though the body doesn't anymore need the calories.

In a 2010 study published in the Current Opinion in Gastroenterology, it was proven that food addiction happens as a result of changes in a person's neuroanatomy and neurochemistry.

Are you addicted to food? An addiction isn't always easy to identify. However, food addicts exhibit symptoms like obsessive-compulsive disorder, depression, or binge eating. They hide their problems, eat in private, and even hide their food.

The most common signs of addiction to food include overeating at mealtimes, eating at strange times, constant snacking, eating even when full, failed attempts at controlling their eating or eliminating bingeing episodes, eating to accompany other activities like talking on the phone or watching TV, associating food with rewards or punishments, and having feelings of shame or guilt after bingeing.

Food addiction may seem harmless compared to other addictions, but it's not. It's a condition that progresses gradually. It eventually results in obesity and/or other health problems while at the same time worsening mental health issues.

What are the treatments for food addiction? This type of addiction is usually treated like any other form of addiction as all addictions work the same way regardless of the subject of addiction. Treatments usually involve changing the behavior while at the same time managing the cravings. Some of the most useful treatments include Cognitive Behavioral Therapy, psychotherapy, nutritional therapies, and 12-step programs like Overeaters Anonymous and Food Addicts Anonymous.

Compulsive Eating & Fixing It

Do NOT confuse compulsive eating with food cravings. These are two different dieting aspects that tend to have almost similar effects on the human body. In simple definition, compulsive eating is an addiction to food. Unlike overeating, this is a disorder that bears some adverse psychological effects on the human body. This is a disorder that can result into overweight and at the same time cause a series of mental and emotional complications.

Remember that if the condition is identified early enough, this is a disorder that can be easily curbed. The very initial sign that can help you identify a potent compulsive eating disorder is uncontrollable eating or binge eating. This means that even after a meal, an individual will go ahead to look for another meal even with a full stomach. Another sign that can help identify potential compulsive eating is the frequent use of laxatives after taking a particular meal. This is a disorder that can cause an individual to take extreme actions to remove the food in the stomach. An individual can engage in some very rigorous exercise or force vomiting so as to create space for extra food intake.

Compulsive eating is a disorder that can have some very hazardous effects on the body. It can lead to complications which can be fatal. One effect of compulsive eating is that it can result into hypertension because of the weight concerns that arise from the excessive eating habit. This is a dieting disorder that can result in some undesired emotional conflicts that can only be settled by food. Compulsive eating is a habit that can begin as early as childhood and result into a change in one's eating habits and patterns. Medical practitioners have proven that compulsive eating is a disorder that mostly occurs in people who use food as a therapy to ease some of their daily problems such as loneliness and frustrations.

Stopping compulsive eating can be quite difficult but the truth is that its remedy lies in the subconscious mind. This means that you must trigger your mind not to use food as a way to compensate for some of the body problems. Compulsive eating can also be stopped by correcting one's self-sabotaging behavior and maintaining an appropriate organic balance of your body needs. Psychiatrists have proven that compulsive eating can be stopped by programming the brain to stop signaling for food whenever there are some unfulfilled desires.

Printed in Great Britain
by Amazon